Employee's Survival Guide to Change

The complete guide to surviving and thriving during organizational change

Jeffrey M. Hiatt

Prosci Learning Center Publications
www.change-management.com

Contents

Introduction

Change can happen at any time to anyone. When change happens to someone else, it can be fascinating to talk about. However, when change happens to you, it can be worrisome and uncomfortable. You may be uncertain about what lies ahead. You may have concerns about job security, increasing workloads, finances or learning new skills.

Most employees who find themselves the targets of change experience these same feelings. What many employees don't know is that they play a key role in the success of change. More importantly, the more informed you are, the more likely you will survive the change and advance professionally in a changing environment.

So, what does it take to be a survivor in today's rapidly changing companies?

1. A solid understanding of the change process and your role in it

2. Answers to questions that will help you succeed

3. A set of tools to help you manage change and reach the outcome you want

As an employee facing the uncertainty of change, one of the most important things you can do is to take time to read this guidebook. Insightful sug-

3

gestions resulting from research with more than 2600 organizations over a 14-year period waits for you in the following pages. The key to professional and personal success during change is in your hands!

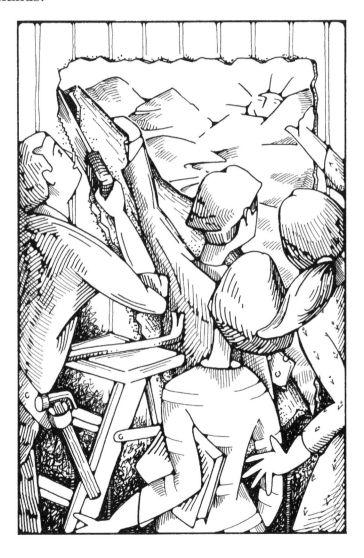

Part 1:
Frequently Asked Questions
(FAQs) About Change

Why is change happening now?

You may feel like change is happening all of a sudden and that it is directed right at you. In reality, most changes begin outside the company many months or even years before internal changes take place. Research shows that most major business changes are responses to changes in the external marketplace.

These external marketplace changes can result in:

- Loss of market share (your company is losing money).

- New offers or capabilities by competitors (they're creating new business faster than your company).

- Lower prices (their cost of doing business is lower, resulting in better prices to their customers).

- A new business opportunity for growth.

External business drivers take time to set in. If they have already affected the bottom line of your company, change is needed immediately. In some cases, it is already too late — the internal change should have started much sooner.

What is the risk of not changing?

When external marketplace changes become apparent inside the organization, managers suddenly realize the risks of not changing.

For businesses, the risk of not changing could mean:

- Loss of jobs (even at the executive level).
- Failure in the marketplace.
- Bankruptcy or loss of revenue.

For employees, the risk of not changing could mean:

- Job dissatisfaction.
- Fewer promotional opportunities.
- Lower job security in the long term.
- Immediate loss of employment.

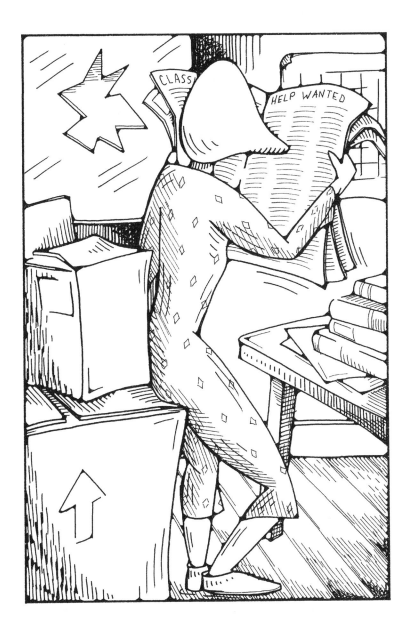

What is the rush?

Employees usually find out what is happening after the fact. Organizations do not always share financial information or talk about poor performance issues with employees. Therefore, when change is needed quickly, employees may be taken by surprise.

> *On one hand, organizations are trying to implement change as quickly as possible; while on the other hand, employees are one step behind trying to understand why the change is needed and how they will be impacted.*

Unfortunately for the company, most employees are in no hurry to change. In fact, many employees may not see the need to change at all. Forcing employees to change when they do not understand the business reasons can be a lot like pushing a giant cube of JELL-O® — you might have an impact, but no real overall shift occurs.

When the force is removed, everything returns to the way it was before.

If I wait long enough, will the change just go away?

If financial success of the organization depends on change, then you can expect the change to happen with or without you. Waiting will usually not change the outcome.

> *In most cases, a company will change — even in the face of resistance from employees — especially if financial success is at stake.*

This does not imply that change will be bad for you. In the end, many changes result in positive outcomes for employees. Benefits might include better tools, improved work processes, more secure jobs and new opportunities for you to advance your career.

What will change mean to me?

Change to a business can include:

- New ways of doing work

- New systems or tools

- New reporting structures

- New job roles

- New products or services

- New markets or geographic locations

The way you are impacted by the change depends on your current job, the extent of the change and the choices you make in response to the change.

With small changes, you may not be impacted at all. With major changes, you may be doing new work, using new tools or reporting to a new manager. With radical changes to the business, some employees may work in other departments or even move to other companies.

When the change is implemented, each person will be affected differently. In the end, how you react to the change plays an important role in how the change will impact you.

The good news is:

You are not a victim of change. Change involves personal decisions and the actions you take will have a direct impact on the outcome you experience.

In other words, you are in control of how you respond to change. Better yet, how the organization views you and your future role in the company may depend on your reaction to change and the choices you make.

16

What is my role?

Your decisions about how to respond to change will vary as the organization moves through the change process. Think about the change in these time periods:

When the change is first announced, but before the change is implemented.

During the change process when the new solution is being deployed.

After the change is in place following the implementation of the solution.

Your choices and their consequences depend on which phase your organization is in. The following pages provide potential actions you may take and the likely outcomes of those actions.

In some cases, decisions you make may have negative outcomes. They may be bad for you and for the company. Other choices you make will benefit you and enhance your ability to thrive in a changing organization.

18

The actions shown on the following pages are separated into:

- Actions with typically negative outcomes

- Actions with typically positive outcomes

These examples help illustrate the conscious and unconscious decisions we all make regarding change.

| Current | Before the change | **Actions that typically have a negative outcome** |

Actions you can take before the change that typically have a negative outcome:

1. Talk badly about the proposed change with your peers or subordinates.

2. Talk negatively about the organization or people in the organization.

3. Talk one way in public, but say otherwise in private conversations.

4. Stop performing your current responsibilities or perform them carelessly.

5. Have secret meetings with your subordinates where the change is minimized or not taken seriously.

Current | **Before the change** | **Actions that typically have a positive outcome**

Actions you can take before the change that typically have a positive outcome:

1. Learn about the change.

2. Ask how you can help.

3. Find out how you can prepare for the change.

4. Display a positive outlook.

5. Encourage constructive conversations with fellow employees.

6. Be open and honest with your feedback about the change.

7. Be quiet and observe. This choice is acceptable during the early phases of a change.

Transition

During the change | **Actions that typically have a negative outcome**

Actions you can take during the change that typically have a negative outcome:

1. Block progress or sabotage the change process.

2. Talk negatively about the change in private conversations.

3. Ignore the change — pretend that it is not happening (denial).

4. Prevent others from participating in the design of the solution or implementation of the change.

Transition	**During the change**	

Actions that typically have a positive outcome

Actions you can take during the change that typically have a positive outcome:

1. Ask questions about the future.

2. Ask how the change will impact day-to-day operations.

3. Provide input to the solution.

4. Find out what new skills and abilities you will need to perform effectively after the change is in place.

5. Assess your own strengths and weaknesses.

6. Seek training that will be available to fill skill gaps.

7. Take advantage of the change to develop new skills and grow professionally.

Future | After the change | # Actions that typically have a negative outcome

Actions you can take after the change that typically have a negative outcome:

1. Avoid using the new work processes or tools whenever possible.

2. Tell peers or subordinates that using the new work processes or tools is not a big deal and shouldn't be taken too seriously.

3. Talk negatively about the organization with customers.

4. Revert to the old way of doing things when problems or issues arise with the change.

5. Take advantage of problems during implementation to argue why the change will never work.

		Actions that typically have a positive outcome
Future	After the change	

Actions you can take after the change that typically have a positive outcome:

1. Reinforce the change with peers and subordinates.

2. Help the business achieve the objectives of the change (be results-oriented).

3. Avoid reverting back to old processes or ways of doing work when problems arise with the new processes and systems.

4. Help solve problems that arise with new work processes and tools.

What are the consequences of not changing?

The consequences to you of not changing depend on how critical the change is to the business.

For changes that are less critical to business success, the consequences may be minimal. However, if you elect not to support a change that is critical to the success of the organization, the likely consequences are:

1. Loss of employment.

2. Reassignment or transfer with the potential for lower pay.

3. Lost opportunities for promotion or advancement in the organization.

4. Reduced job satisfaction as you fight the organization and the organization fights you.

What are the benefits of supporting the change?

The benefits of supporting the change, especially changes that are critical to the success of the organization, include:

1. Enhanced respect and reputation within the organization.

2. Improved growth opportunities (especially for active supporters of the change).

3. Increased job satisfaction (knowing you are helping your organization respond effectively to a rapidly changing marketplace).

4. Improved job security.

What if I disagree with the change? What if I feel they are fixing the wrong problem?

Be patient. Keep an open mind. Make sure you understand the business reasons for the change. However, don't be afraid to voice your specific objections or concerns. If your objections are valid, chances are good they will come to light and be resolved. If you feel strongly against a specific element of the change, let the right people know and do it in an appropriate manner.

What if they've tried before and failed?

The history of your company may include some previous change projects that have failed. If failure is what employees are accustomed to, the organization will have a hard time erasing the past. In order for companies to be successful, everyone must be prepared to accept the past as history and focus on what lies ahead.

What if I am forced to do more for the same pay?

When your organization is undergoing a change, this usually means that new processes, systems or skills are required. Your role in the changed environment may include learning these new processes or acquiring new skills. Indeed, some of your responsibilities may change.

For the old way of doing things, compensation may actually decrease as the value of that work to the organization goes down. However, compensation for new work may increase as the value for new services and products increases. This is a part of change.

Part 2:
Taking Control of Change

The Prosci® ADKAR® Model

Research with more than 2600 companies over 14 years resulted in a model for managing change called the ADKAR Model.[1]

ADKAR represents the five building blocks of change that must be achieved for a change to be a success. By using this model you can:

- Determine where you are in the change process.

- Create a successful action plan for personal and professional advancement through the change process.

In this section, the ADKAR Model is presented along with several case studies. Following the case study examples, worksheets are provided that will allow you to apply this model to a change occurring in your personal life and at work. By applying the model you will be able to identify any barriers to change, diagnose why a change may not be working and make decisions about how to most effectively deal with the change.

This model is also useful to apply in personal and home situations. The ADKAR Model is helpful to facilitate change whether you are the target of the change or if you are the one wanting to make a change happen.

---

1. ADKAR and "Awareness, Desire, Knowledge, Ability, Reinforcement" are registered trademarks of Prosci Inc.

The ADKAR Model has five stages:

- **Awareness** of the need for change

- **Desire** to make the change happen

- **Knowledge** about how to change

- **Ability** to implement new skills and behaviors

- **Reinforcement** to retain the change once it has been made

Prosci® **ADKAR**® **Model**	**Awareness** **Desire** **Knowledge** **Ability** **Reinforcement**®

When faced with change, your task is to determine where you fall in this model and then ask yourself, "What does this change mean to me?"

This type of critical thinking directs energy at the most important component of change. If you can do this successfully, you will have a much clearer view of your options for dealing with change and be better prepared to interact with your work colleagues and management.

Take a minute to look at the model more closely. In the following examples, we examine a simple work scenario and a personal case study. After reviewing these examples, you can complete the worksheets for both a personal change and a change happening at work.

ADKAR Stage	Considerations
Awareness of the need for change	• What is the nature of the change? • Why is the change needed? • What is the risk of not changing?
Desire to make the change happen	• What's in it for me (WIIFM)? • A personal choice • A decision to engage and participate
Knowledge about how to change	• Understanding how to change • Training on new processes and tools • Learning new skills
Ability to implement new skills and behaviors	• The demonstrated capability to implement the change • Achievement of the desired change in performance or behavior
Reinforcement to retain the change once it is made	• Actions that increase the likelihood that a change will be continued • Recognition and rewards that sustain the change

A first look at the model: ADKAR applied to a work scenario

In this first example, a department is implementing a new software tool for customer records. For the purpose of this example, put yourself in the position of a long-tenured customer service employee in this department. If the change is implemented and you believe it was not needed (i.e., you were not aware that any changes were required), then your reaction might be:

"This is a waste of time."

"If it ain't broke, don't fix it."

"They never tell us what's going on!"

The natural reaction to change, even in the best circumstances, is to resist. Awareness of the business need to change is a critical ingredient of any change and must come first.

Awareness includes understanding why the change is happening, what will happen if the change is not made and what business conditions created a need for this change. If someone had taken the time to explain that the old software would no longer be supported by the vendor, and that the new software was necessary to meet the needs of your customers, then your reaction (based on this awareness) would likely be very different:

"How soon will this happen?"

"How will this impact me?"

Take this same example one step further. If you were aware that a change was required and had the desire to support the change, then the next logical step is to seek knowledge about the change and the skills necessary to implement the change.

"How will the new process work?"

"Will I receive training on the new tools?"

Once you have obtained the necessary knowledge, then you will need practice to develop the ability to implement the new processes and new skills on the job. Coaching, mentoring and simply having time to practice are key elements for developing ability.

Finally, reinforcement is necessary to recognize and reward a successful change. Celebrating success can help make a change stick.

In this example, you assumed the role of an employee who was the target of change. In the next example, view the change from the perspective of a parent who is trying to motivate their child to change.

ADKAR applied to coaching a sport

Dad was attempting to improve the batting style and skill of his son playing baseball. He was concerned that his son's batting was not up to the level of the other boys on the team. After observing his son's batting for several games, Dad decided to take action. He searched the internet for batting videos and bookmarked one for his son.

For weeks he tried to get his son to watch the video on batting mechanics. With some parental persuasion and pressure, Dad was able to get his son to watch only a few minutes. After that, the video was left untouched. The son's batting performance remained unchanged.

The father's attempt to change his son's batting performance was failing and producing only frustration. He finally sat down with his son and asked him why he would not watch the video and use it to improve his batting.

His son replied that he just enjoyed playing baseball with his friends and it did not matter to him if his batting was as good as some of the other boys. He commented that he already knew what to do, but just had problems making it happen.

If you break down this case study into the five parts of the ADKAR Model, you can quickly identify where the dad's efforts failed.

1. **Does this player have awareness of his performance gap?** In this case, the player's performance at batting is visible to everyone on the team, including himself. On a scale of 1 to 5, with 5 being the most aware, he might be ranked a 5.

2. **Does this player have a desire to improve his performance?** He does not demonstrate a strong internal motivation to improve his batting and most of the pressure is coming from his dad. On a scale of 1 to 5, the player would most likely rank a 1 or 2.

3. **Does this player have the knowledge to implement a change in batting style and performance?** Based on the boy's comments to his father, he did understand batting techniques. For knowledge, he likely would rank a 3 or 4.

4. **Does this player have the ability to implement this knowledge?** The player's ability to implement improved batting techniques is low based on his difficulty putting the knowledge into practice, and would probably rank a 1 or 2 on a scale of 5.

5. **Does this player receive reinforcement for improved batting?** Since batting ability remains low, no reinforcement is present and would rank a 1 on a scale of 5.

The ADKAR score for this example is:

Awareness - 5
Desire - 1
Knowledge - 4
Ability - 1
Reinforcement - 1

Note that desire is the first low score. The first score of 3 or below in the ADKAR Model is referred to as the **barrier point** to change. The barrier point must be the first area addressed in order for change to be successful.

In this example, the father skipped steps in the ADKAR Model and missed the barrier point to change. He skipped from **awareness** to **knowledge**, even though his son had no **desire** to change. He was simply content just to be out there playing the game. Dad's efforts to build **knowledge and ability** failed because his son lacked the **desire** to change.

Every change has a different barrier point. In this coaching example, it was **desire**. In the previous example for the new software tool, the barrier point was **awareness**. Whether dealing with a personal change or a business change, the challenge is to find the barrier point.

Once that barrier point is identified, you can begin to constructively deal with the change.

Identifying the barrier point

ADKAR worksheets can help identify the barrier point for your change. To practice, first apply this simple process to a personal situation. Begin by identifying a change you would like to support in another person, but up to now all your efforts have been unsuccessful. This change could be with a friend, family member or work associate. Complete the following worksheets to the best of your ability, rating each area on a scale of 1 to 5. Be sure you select a change, which you have been trying to facilitate in a friend, colleague or family member, that is not working regardless of your continued efforts. You will be evaluating the following questions:

To what degree is this person **aware** of the need for change?

Does this person have a **desire** to change?

Do they have the required **knowledge** and skills to support the change?

Do they have the **ability** to act on this knowledge and make the change happen?

Do they have the necessary **reinforcement** in place to sustain the change?

Use the worksheets provided on the following pages to note your observations.

Introduction

Briefly describe the **personal** change you are trying to implement with a friend, family member or work associate.

_____

_____

_____

_____

_____

_____

_____

_____

_____

_____

_____

_____

_____

_____

_____

_____

_____

_____

_____

_____

_____

_____

_____

_____

_____

1. List the reasons you believe the change is necessary.

_____

_____

_____

_____

_____

_____

_____

_____

_____

_____

_____

_____

_____

_____

Review these reasons and ask yourself the degree to which this person is aware of these reasons. Rate their **awareness** on a scale of 1 to 5.

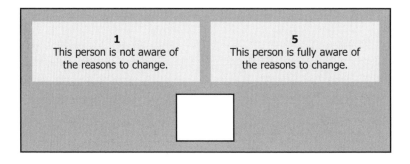

1	**5**
This person is not aware of the reasons to change.	This person is fully aware of the reasons to change.

2. List the factors or consequences (good and bad) that create a desire to change for this person.

_____

_____

_____

_____

_____

_____

_____

_____

_____

_____

_____

_____

_____

_____

_____

_____

_____

Consider these motivating factors, including the person's conviction in these factors and the associated consequences. Rate their **desire** to change on a scale of 1 to 5.

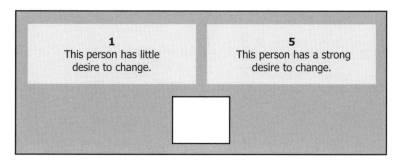

1	5
This person has little desire to change.	This person has a strong desire to change.

3. List the skills and knowledge needed for the change.

_____

_____

_____

_____

_____

_____

_____

_____

_____

_____

_____

_____

_____

_____

_____

_____

Rate this person's **knowledge** or training in these areas on a scale of 1 to 5.

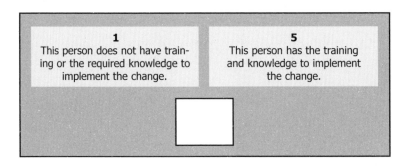

1	**5**
This person does not have training or the required knowledge to implement the change.	This person has the training and knowledge to implement the change.

4. Considering the skills and knowledge identified in Step 3, evaluate the person's ability to perform these skills or act on this knowledge.

_____

_____

_____

_____

_____

_____

_____

_____

_____

_____

_____

_____

_____

_____

_____

_____

Rate this person's **ability** to implement the new skills, knowledge and behaviors to support the change on a scale of 1 to 5.

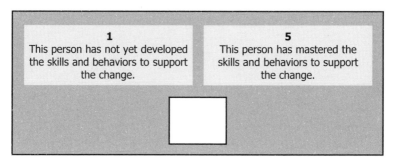

1	**5**
This person has not yet developed the skills and behaviors to support the change.	This person has mastered the skills and behaviors to support the change.

5. List the reinforcements that will help to retain the change. Are incentives in place to reinforce the change and make it stick?

_____

_____

_____

_____

_____

_____

_____

_____

_____

_____

_____

_____

_____

_____

_____

_____

Rate the degree to which this person is receiving *reinforcement* for demonstrating the change on a scale of 1 to 5.

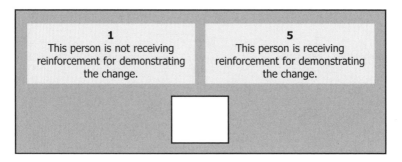

1	5
This person is not receiving reinforcement for demonstrating the change.	This person is receiving reinforcement for demonstrating the change.

Now transfer your scores from each worksheet to the table shown in Figure 1 on the next page. Take a moment to review your scores. Highlight those areas that scored a 3 or below and identify (using the order listed on the scoresheet) which was the **first** area to score a 3 or below (the barrier point). Note that in the example worksheet in Figure 2, **desire** was the first area in the coaching example to score a 3 or below.

Brief description of the change: _____ _____	Rank
1. *Awareness* of the need to change? Notes:_____	
2. *Desire* to make the change happen? Notes:_____	
3. *Knowledge* about how to change? Notes:_____	
4. *Ability* to change? Notes:_____	
5. *Reinforcement* to retain the change? Notes:_____	

Figure 1 - Change evaluation worksheet

Brief description of the change: Improve batting	Rank
1. *Awareness* of the need to change? Notes:_____	*5*
2. *Desire* to make the change happen? Notes:_____	(*1*)
3. *Knowledge* about how to change? Notes:_____	*4*
4. *Ability* to change? Notes:_____	*1*
5. *Reinforcement* to retain the change? Notes:_____	*1*

Figure 2 - Sample evaluation worksheet

Now consider the first area in which the score was a 3 or below. *This is defined as the barrier point for this change.* You must address this area before anything else is done. For example, if you identified **awareness** as the barrier point, then working on desire, knowledge or skill development will not help make the change happen.

On the other hand, if you identified **desire**, then continually repeating your reasons for change is not adequate to move this person forward. Once they know these reasons, you must address their inherent desire to change. Desire may stem from negative or positive consequences. The negative consequences have to be great enough to overcome their personal threshold to resist change (same for the positive consequences).

If **knowledge** was the barrier point, then you want to be careful not to dwell on the reasons for change and the motivating factors. This could be discouraging for someone already at this phase. What is needed is education and training for the skills and behaviors that are needed for change.

If **ability** was the first area with a score of 3 or below, then several elements may be required to move forward:

- The person will need time to develop the new skills and behaviors. With any new skill, time is required to develop new abilities.

54

- The person will need ongoing coaching and support. No one-time training event or educational program will substitute for ongoing coaching and mentoring.

- Physical or psychological barriers may require special interventions to be removed.

Finally, if **reinforcement** was the area identified, then you will need to investigate if the necessary elements are present to keep the person from reverting to old behaviors.

Now that you have completed the ADKAR Model for a personal change, you can follow the same process for a change happening at work. This process will give you insight to where you are in the change process and help you identify if you have a barrier point to change.

The ADKAR Model allows you to identify, put in order and focus on the critical elements of your change initiative. When you approach change using this model, you can immediately identify where the process is breaking down and which elements are being overlooked. This avoids generic conversations about the change that rarely produce actionable steps. Finding your **barrier point** can help you diagnose why a current change is failing and focus your energy and conversation on the area that will most likely produce progress and ultimately success.

In most cases, where the ADKAR Model is applied and the barrier point identified, corrective action can be taken and the change successfully implemented. However, that is not always the case. In some instances, a person is making a conscious decision not to change (i.e., they have no desire to participate in the change). In other cases, a person may have a physical or mental condition that simply prevents them from developing the ability to change. The ADKAR Model helps identify these barriers quickly.

Here are the five steps again:

- **Awareness** of the need for change

- **Desire** to make the change happen

- **Knowledge** about how to change

- **Ability** to implement new skills and behaviors

- **Reinforcement** to retain the change once it has been made

The following worksheets can be used for business changes. Where is your barrier point for the change happening at work? After you have completed these worksheets, you can create an ADKAR profile for this change (profile examples are provided in the pages following the worksheets).

Business change

Briefly describe the change that is being implemented at your company.

_____

_____

_____

_____

_____

_____

_____

_____

_____

_____

_____

_____

_____

_____

_____

_____

_____

_____

_____

_____

_____

1. Describe your awareness of the need to change. What are the business, customer or competitor issues that have created a need to change?

_____

_____

_____

_____

_____

_____

_____

_____

_____

_____

_____

_____

_____

_____

_____

_____

Rate your **awareness** of the need to change on a scale of 1 to 5.

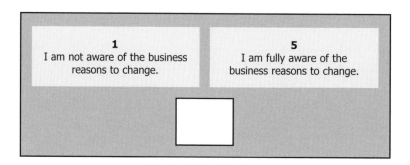

1 I am not aware of the business reasons to change.	**5** I am fully aware of the business reasons to change.

2. List the factors or consequences (good and bad) related to this change that affect your desire to change.

_____
_____
_____
_____
_____
_____
_____
_____
_____
_____
_____
_____
_____
_____
_____
_____
_____

Consider these motivating factors. Rate your over-all *desire* to change on a scale of 1 to 5.

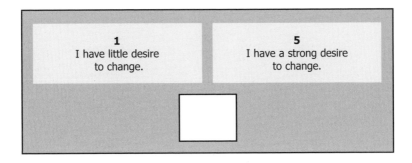

1	5
I have little desire to change.	I have a strong desire to change.

3. List the skills and knowledge needed to support this change.

_____

_____

_____

_____

_____

_____

_____

_____

_____

_____

_____

_____

_____

_____

Do you have a clear understanding of the change and the skills you will need to operate in the new environment? Have you received education or training to learn these skills? Rate your **knowledge** of how to change on a scale of 1 to 5.

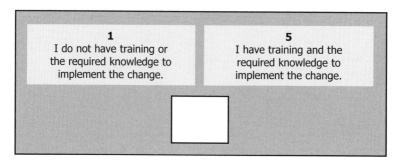

1	5
I do not have training or the required knowledge to implement the change.	I have training and the required knowledge to implement the change.

4. Considering the skills and knowledge identified in Step 3, assess your overall ability in each area (low, medium, high).

_____

_____

_____

_____

_____

_____

_____

_____

_____

_____

_____

_____

_____

_____

_____

_____

Review your evaluations and rate your overall _ability_ to change on a scale of 1 to 5.

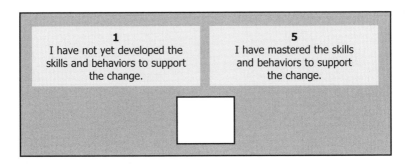

1	5
I have not yet developed the skills and behaviors to support the change.	I have mastered the skills and behaviors to support the change.

5. List the reinforcements that will help retain the change. Are incentives in place to reinforce the change and make it stick?

_____

_____

_____

_____

_____

_____

_____

_____

_____

_____

_____

_____

_____

_____

_____

_____

Rate the degree to which you are receiving **rein-forcement** for demonstrating the change on a scale of 1 to 5.

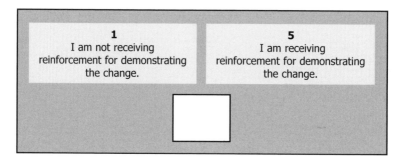

1	5
I am not receiving reinforcement for demonstrating the change.	I am receiving reinforcement for demonstrating the change.

Transfer your scores from the worksheets to the table below. Circle the first area where you scored a 3 or below.

Brief description of the change:	Rank
_____ _____	
1. *Awareness* of the need to change? Notes:_____	
2. *Desire* to make the change happen? Notes:_____	
3. *Knowledge* about how to change? Notes:_____	
4. *Ability* to change? Notes:_____	
5. *Reinforcement* to retain the change? Notes:_____	

Analyzing ADKAR

Based on your scores in this exercise you can create an ADKAR profile. Two examples are shown below. The first example shows that desire is the barrier point. In this example, you would address "desire" first using the guidelines described on page 66. The second example below shows that "ability" is the first ADKAR element with a low score (3 or less). In this case, you would address "ability" first. The insight from these profiles is recognizing the ADKAR element that is your barrier point to change and focusing on that area first.

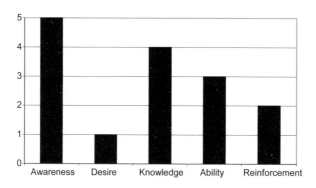

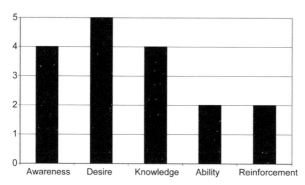

Barrier Point: Awareness
Action Steps

**Ask your manager or members of the
change management team
the following questions:**

- What are the benefits and business reasons for the change?

- What is happening inside the business or external to the business that is creating the need to change?

- How do these external or internal drivers impact the business, our organization, our department and me as an employee?

- What do our customers want or expect that is creating a need for change?

- What are our competitors doing that is creating a need for change?

- What will happen if a change is not made?

- How will the change take place and what will the future state look like?

- What can I expect to happen and when?

Barrier Point: Desire
Action Steps

To know what steps to take, first determine which group you are in:

Group 1:

You are motivated to change simply by understanding what is happening to the business (i.e., what was discussed in the awareness step). You need very little, if any, incentive beyond this basic knowledge. You are a willing participant and active supporter of the change.

Group 2:

You are neutral or cautious about the change. You may need incentives, personal attention or definitive consequences for supporting or not supporting the change. You will need to understand how the change will impact you personally (what is in it for you). You will need to understand the risk to the organization and yourself if a change is not made.

Group 3:

You will not support the change no matter what is done. You will either openly obstruct the effort or leave the company. You may be a passive observer but behind the scenes you actively campaign against the change.

Desire action steps continued

If you are in Group 1:
(Already supportive of the change)

- Help deploy the change

- Participate on extended teams to support detailed design activities

- Help develop training or help test new systems and tools

- Act as a mentor and coach to other employees

Desire action steps continued

If you are in Group 2:
(Unsure about the change)

- Be patient. You may need time to sort out the change and the impact on you.

- Continually seek information on the business needs and changing environment.

- Learn the risks to the business if a change is not made. Determine how the change will impact you personally.

- Have direct communications with a coach or supervisor that understands the change and can communicate the business reasons behind it, as well as the impact on you.

- Voice your objections to the change and understand why those objections cannot be satisfied, or help the design team modify the solution to account for these objections.

- Understand the personal consequences of not changing and talk candidly with your supervisor about your choices.

68

Desire action steps continued

If you are in Group 3:
(Outright opposed to the change)

If you chose Group 3, you should talk to your supervisor to understand the consequences of that decision. Determine if you are possibly in Group 2 and just need your concerns listened to and addressed.

Alternatively, this may be the time to explore other work opportunities. Finding work that fits your personal and professional development goals is a critical step for individuals involved in major change initiatives, especially when the direction of the organization is different than the goals of an individual.

Barrier Point: Knowledge
Action Steps

Seek information from your manager or the change management team about training and educational opportunities. Attend meetings and presentations about the change. Be active in asking questions and seeking out more information.

You should actively pursue the following information during the change process:

- Clear definition of the change

- Education and training opportunities

- Information about how the change will impact you

- New performance measures

Clear definition of the change

Each element of the change, including new business processes, new technology or tools, organizational impacts and changes in job roles, should be clearly defined and explained. However, be patient. For some changes, these take time to develop.

Knowledge action steps continued

Education and training

Training programs or information should be available for each area of the change, including how to use new systems, tools and business processes. Again, be patient. Much of the information and training will be developed along with the change.

How the change will impact you

Seek out information that explains how the change will impact you and what is expected from you, including:

"How will this change impact my work?"

"What will change for me on a daily basis?"

"What new skills or knowledge do I need?"

New performance measures

New measures and expectations for performance should be clearly defined and communicated to everyone.

71

Barrier Point: Ability
Action Steps

Change is a process. Developing the ability to change means adopting new habits and learning new skills. This takes time. Simply attending training courses is not enough. You will need ongoing support mechanisms and coaching.

In the changed environment, you will encounter circumstances that don't match what you learned in training. In these situations you may be tempted to revert to "the old way of doing things" because of the uncertainty of change.

Instead, raise the issue to your supervisor or change management team and help work through problems with the new design.

Continually work to develop the new skills and behaviors that are required to support the change. When gaps persist, seek additional training to close these gaps.

Ability action steps continued

You can use various methods to build new skills and behaviors:

- Monitor your own performance and check yourself against the objectives of the change. Seek help when they don't match. Write down your own goals and take steps to achieve those objectives.

- Attend ongoing training and educational programs in areas where you have skill gaps.

- Be patient. It takes time to develop new habits and learn new ways of doing work. Be persistent, positive and results-oriented.

73

Barrier Point: Reinforcement
Action Steps

Reinforcing the change is just as important as implementing it. Our natural tendency is to revert to "the old way of doing things." Every individual plays a role in reinforcing the new way of doing work.

Seek support from your supervisor when the process does not work correctly. Help solve the problems that arise while using new tools and processes. Avoid using old processes when the new processes are not working. Raise issues and make sure they are escalated quickly to the right people.

ADKAR Summary

Prosci® Awareness
Desire
ADKAR® Knowledge
Ability
Model Reinforcement®

Change opens new doors and new opportunities for both you and the organization. You can take advantage of change to develop professionally and move forward in the organization.

Every business is undergoing change. It is part of today's workplace. Learning how to survive and thrive in a changing environment is a critical skill for advancement and growth.

No change comes without some pain. Certainly, the goal is to minimize that pain and implement the change as quickly as possible. More importantly, you can thrive in a changing environment by using the Prosci® ADKAR® Model as a practical tool to understand and manage change.

You are no longer a "victim" of change but an active member in helping make change successful. Use your understanding of change and tools like ADKAR to help you be successful with changes both at work and at home.

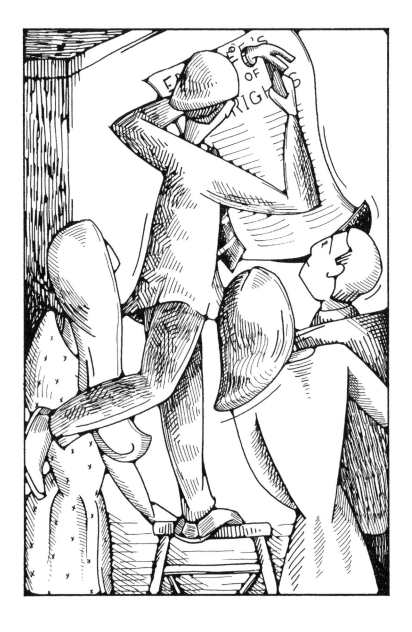

Part 3:
Highlights and Tips

Gaining perspective on change

This section provides highlights and puts in perspective topics covered to this point. Also provided are tips for using the tools with your group or department. The purpose of this section is to provide a quick review of the key concepts and suggest ways you can take positive steps to manage the change process.

Change is a process

Change is a movement out of a current state (how things are today), through a transition state, to a future state (how things will be done). Comfort with the current state and fear of the unknown future may cause resistance — this is normal.

Change starts from the outside

Nearly all fundamental change taking place within an organization is a response to external stimulus from customers, competitors or market conditions. In most cases financial performance, or the lack thereof, is a critical driver of these changes.

Risk of not changing

Organizations that do not respond to marketplace changes risk customer dissatisfaction, declining market share and poor financial performance. This can apply to both public and private-sector organizations. The viability of the organization is at risk, as well as the jobs of executives, managers and front-line employees.

What's the hurry?

Typically, too much time elapses between the time the organization feels the pain of outside market influences and the time that change initiatives reach front-line managers and employees. The result is that change was needed yesterday. Meetings and more meetings can become commonplace as the organization reacts to change.

You have a role

At each step of the change process, you have decisions to make that impact your role and how others perceive you. Each of these actions has consequences, which in many cases you can predict ahead of time. Every conversation you have, whether in meetings or around the coffee pot, reflects your choices about change.

Choices and accountability

Change can be traumatic for everyone involved, even when the final result may be positive. In the end, each person must choose whether they will change or remain the same. We are each accountable for our choices and actions related to change. Adopting this frame of mind will help prevent you from becoming a victim of change.

Taking control of change

You can take control of the change process and how that process impacts you personally and professionally. The ADKAR Model provides a concrete action plan for assessing where you are in the change process, which steps you can take to fill in the missing puzzle pieces, and how you can move ahead.

Tips for group activities

The worksheets provided with the ADKAR Model are effective to use with groups or teams. They can stimulate conversation and provide a basis for discussion that will help your team navigate the change process.

Group activities

Team size of fewer than six

For groups with fewer than six members, have each member complete the ADKAR worksheets for the change occurring in the organization. Then have the members bring their final score sheets to the group meeting.

As a group, complete the worksheets using a flip chart. In this process, you should repeat the same process you used individually, but use the collective input from the group. Then create a group scorecard.

Now compare personal scores with the group scores. Discuss as a group why any differences or similarities exist with how you rated each area of the ADKAR Model. Create an action plan for each person and for the group as a whole.

To assist in these activities, worksheets are available at www.change-management.com or by calling Prosci at +1 (970) 203-9332.

Team size of six or more

By following these steps, teams of six or more can facilitate a large group session with great results.

1. Have members of the group complete the worksheets on their own.

2. Bring together the entire team and divide the group into smaller teams of two or three members each. Avoid having groups with more than four members per team.

3. Have each sub-team break out into separate rooms, or separate areas of a larger room, and use a flip chart to complete the ADKAR worksheets as a group.

4. Once complete (after about 45 minutes), bring the teams back together and allow each team to present the highlights of each area of the ADKAR Model.

5. Compare the scores from the final score sheets of each team, and identify patterns and themes for each area.

Be sure to designate someone to take notes and document the findings of the group meeting. Assign a group of volunteers to create an action plan. Remember that everyone has a role in the change process.

References

Best Practices in Change Management. Prosci Inc., 2012.
Prosci's Best Practices in Change Management *benchmark-
ing report will help you optimize your change management
approach to achieve business results on change projects with
real-world research. The report combines findings over a
14-year period from 2600 organizations from more than 60
countries to present what is working and what is not working in
the field of change management.*

***ADKAR: A model for change in business, government
and our community***. Prosci Inc., 2006.
*In his first complete text on the Prosci® ADKAR® Model, Jeff
Hiatt explains the origin of the model and explores what drives
each building block of ADKAR. Learn how to build awareness,
create desire, develop knowledge, foster ability and reinforce
changes in your organization. The ADKAR Model is changing
how we think about managing the people side of change, and
provides a powerful foundation to help you succeed at change.*

Contact information

Prosci Inc.
Phone: +1 (970) 203-9332
Toll free: +1 (800) 700-2831
Fax: +1 (970) 669-7005
www.prosci.com

Change Management Learning Center
www.change-management.com